Why Do People Make and Sell Drugs?

W
FRANKLIN WATTS
LONDON•SYDNEY

First published in 2010 by Franklin Watts

Franklin Watts
338 Euston Road
London NW1 3BH

Franklin Watts Australia
Level 17/207 Kent Street, Sydney, NSW 2000

Produced by Arcturus Publishing Limited,
26/27 Bickels Yard, 151–153 Bermondsey Street, London SE1 3HA

Series concept: Alex Woolf
Editor and picture researcher: Jonathan Hilton
Designer: Ian Winton

Picture credits:
Corbis: cover (Michael S. Yamashita), title page (Karen Kasmauski), 6 (Julian Smith), 7 (Owen Franken), 8 (Rob Howard), 9 (Gustavo Gilabert/Saba), 11–14 (Bettmann), 15 (Jalil Rezayee/epa), 16 (Jawed Kargar/epa), 17 (Jeffrey L Rotman), 18 (Manca Juvan), 19 (Reuters), 20 (Nathan Benn), 21 (Jacques M Chenet), 22 (Andrew Lichtenstein), 23 (Mika), 24 (Akhtar Gulfam/epa), 25 (Jérôme Sessini), 26 (Ashley Cooper), 27 (Reuters), 28 (Daniel Aguilar/ Reuters), 29 (Patrick Chauvel/Sygma), 30 (Jeffrey L Rotman), 31 (Bob E Daemmrich/Sygma), 32 (Reuters), 33 (Gerd Ludwig), 34 (Kaosot Newspaper/epa), 35 (Gideon Mendel), 36 (Philippe Eranian/Sygma), 37 (Jim McDonald), 38 (Brenda Ann Kenneally), 39 (Janet Jarman), 40 (Owen Franken), 41 (Ann Johansson), 42 (Gideon Mendel), 43 (Michael Dalder/Reuters).

Cover caption: Sap from the seed head of the opium poppy is the raw material for heroin, used by between 15 and 20 million people around the world.
Title page caption: A worker in a marijuana strike force destroying illegal crops in Kentucky, USA.

A CIP catalogue record for this book is available from the British Library.

Dewey Decimal Classification Number: 363.4'5

ISBN 978 1 4451 0069 2

Printed in Singapore

Franklin Watts is a division of Hachette Children's Books, an Hachette UK company.
www.hachettelivre.co.uk

SL001359EN

Contents

Chapter 1

Drugs - what's the deal?

A teenager mourning a dead friend; a farmer shot on his plantation; a tourist facing 20 years in jail; a young man stabbed for a few grams of heroin – all of these people are victims of the worldwide trade in illegal drugs. Fuelled by greed and desperation, the multi-billion-dollar drug industry is one of the hardest problems facing international law enforcement.

What are drugs?

We hear a lot about people 'doing drugs', but what does it mean? What are drugs, where do they come from and why do people deal in and use them?

A drug is any substance that alters your physical or mental state. Drugs range from the caffeine in coffee, tea and cola, through medical drugs, alcohol and tobacco, to street drugs, such as heroin and crack cocaine. Some drugs are legal and can be bought anywhere. Others are illegal and trade in them is a dangerous business. There are around 180–200 million illegal drugs users around the world and trade in drugs is worth more than $300 billion (about £180 billion) a year.

Illegal drugs

There are many popular ideas about how illegal drugs are used. Street drugs such as heroin, crack cocaine and crystal meth

Nightclubs and raves, such as this one in Melbourne, Australia, are frequently venues for drug taking. Some dancers hope to 'keep going' longer and have more fun by using recreational drugs as they party.

In the Netherlands, smoking cannabis is allowed in coffee shops. This young man is lighting a 'bong' – a special pipe for smoking cannabis. The smoke is bubbled through water to cool it before it is inhaled.

(methamphetamine hydrochloride) are often associated with hard-core junkies smoking or injecting in dingy drug dens. This is the common media image of 'hard' drug use, but there are many other illegal drugs that don't fit this picture. 'Dance drugs', such as ecstasy and ketamine, for example, are often used at nightclubs and raves. Some drugs, including LSD, cannabis and magic mushrooms, are more commonly associated with music festivals and the hippy lifestyle. Cocaine is sometimes considered a 'lifestyle' drug, used by fast-living professionals.

These popular images of drug use do not give the complete picture, though. Many drug users are just ordinary people. Their families may not know they use drugs. The users' drug use may be controlled, or it may be dangerous misuse. It is important to bear in mind that both legal and illegal drugs can be misused. The pattern of use and the dangers involved bear little relation to the legal status of the drug. Tobacco contains nicotine, one of the most addictive (habit-forming) substances known. If tobacco were newly discovered today it would probably be classified as illegal in most countries.

Expert View

'Right now, if you ask me would I do it again, I would tell you no because of the suffering of my family. But very few people retire from drug smuggling because once you get your first million, then you want five million. You want ten million. Greed is the name of the game, you know?'

Anonymous drug smuggler

Misuse of drugs

Misusing drugs can have an impact on physical and mental health, and can lead to dependency (also called addiction). Dependency means that people are no longer exercising a free choice in taking the drug. Their use of the drug has led to their bodies craving the substance, so that they take it whether or not they consciously want to.

Drug dependency

Dependency can be physical or psychological. Physical dependence means that the body has become so accustomed to the presence and effects of the drug that the person cannot feel normal or function properly without it. Without the drug, the user suffers physical withdrawal symptoms, such as fever, sickness or aching muscles. Both nicotine and heroin produce physical dependency.

FORUM

There are differing views on how we should tackle drug users – do they need help or should they be pursued by the law?

'People who take drugs need medical help, not criminal retribution.'

Antonio Maria Costa, director of the United Nations Office on Drugs and Crime

'We have to crack down on drug use in our cities and towns.'

US president Barack Obama

What's your opinion?

Coastguards work ceaselessly to stop drugs entering a country by sea, and to prevent the transport of drugs from where they are made or processed to where they will be sold. These Colombian coastguards are seizing a shipment of cocaine bound for the USA.

Peasant farmworkers harvesting coca (the raw material from which cocaine is produced) in the high valley surrounding the town of Quillabamba in Peru.

Psychological dependence is a strong mental habit. The drug user may feel depressed, anxious or jittery without the drug. A person psychologically dependent on a drug such as ecstasy may be drawn to the mental state the drug produces, or they may be desperate for the freedom from misery and anxiety that it brings.

It is the addictive nature of drugs that drives the illegal trade. Around 28 million people around the world are heavy drug users, so there is a ready market for drugs. There will always be people who are willing to take risks and commit crimes in order to provide them.

The drugs trade

Trading in drugs is a dangerous business. Criminal activity and violence are common at all stages of the process. Money from the drugs trade often goes to finance guerrilla wars, terrorism and the activities of violent criminal gangs.

Many drugs are produced in one country, but used in another. This has led to a complex and extensive international trade in drugs. Heroin, for example, is made from opium. Most opium poppies are grown in Afghanistan, but heroin is used around the world. The heroin trade begins with the farmers who grow the poppies and takes in those who process the opium into heroin, those who smuggle the drug around the world, the drug barons who control the trade, and the dealers who sell it on to users. It is a shady, dark world governed by ruthless, greedy people, that makes victims of many ordinary people.

Chapter 2

Have people always used drugs?

Drugs are nothing new. People have used mind-altering substances to produce trances and frenzies in religious rituals for thousands of years. They have also taken drugs for recreation or to escape the misery of their harsh lives.

Drugs through history

People discovered many thousands of years ago that eating, drinking or smoking the leaves or seeds of some plants produced pleasurable physical or mental sensations.

Opium has been used for around 5,400 years. Its use was first recorded by the Sumerians. The ancient Egyptians and Greeks knew and used opium, and the Arabs took it to China nearly 2,000 years ago. In South America people chewed the leaves of the coca plant (the source of cocaine) at least 5,000 years ago. The Spanish invaders of South America took over coca plantations from the Incas in the early sixteenth century and introduced coca to Europe. Within a few years Spanish landowners in South America were even allowed to make their tax payments in coca leaves. By about 1575 around 8 per cent of the Europeans living in Peru were working in the coca trade.

Fighting over drugs

Drugs have been the cause of local skirmishes and international wars in the past, just as they are today. The opium trade has been the cause of international strife for more than 200 years.

Expert View

'To get this heroin supply the addict will . . . lie, steal, rob and if necessary commit murder. Heroin addiction can be likened to a contagion. Suppose it were announced that there were more than a million lepers among our people. Think what a shock the announcement would make. Yet drug addiction is far more incurable than leprosy, far more tragic to its victims, and is spreading like a moral and physical scourge.'

Richard Pearson Hobson, nineteenth-century anti-drug campaigner

British troops in action capturing the city of Zhenjiang on their way to Nanjing (known to the British as Nanking) in 1842 during the First Opium War.

From 1761 the British East India Company controlled the trade in opium grown in India. The British deliberately encouraged opium use in China so that they could export opium to China, against Chinese law. Opium addiction became a grave problem in China with the effects on the population becoming progressively worse. In 1838 China began a crackdown, stopping British boats and seizing and destroying opium. The British responded with violence, which escalated into war. The Opium Wars ended in humiliation for China. Under the Treaty of Nanking (1842), the Chinese paid the British a vast sum in compensation and surrendered Hong Kong. The island remained under British rule until 1997.

Continuing battles

Drugs are still a cause of conflict. In Afghanistan the powerful militant political and religious group, the Taliban, uses guerrilla tactics to fight against the enforcers of the government's opium-eradication programme. In South America and Asia, violent skirmishes over drug farms and shipments are common.

Chemistry yields new drugs

For hundreds of years people used drugs from plants such as coca and tobacco in their raw form, just chewing or smoking them. They used simple techniques to brew alcohol and to extract opium from poppies. Then, in the nineteenth century, developments in the science of chemistry led to new types of drug.

In 1804 the German scientist Friedrich Sertürner discovered the active ingredient in opium. He dissolved sap from opium poppies in hot water and added ammonia to obtain crystals of the alkaloid morphine. This was the first time an active ingredient had been extracted and it marked the start of the modern pharmaceutical industry.

The medical use of morphine as a painkiller grew rapidly, but morphine is addictive. From 1898 it was replaced by heroin, which was advertised – wrongly as we now know – as being non-addictive. Morphine and heroin were readily and legally available, as was cocaine. Indeed, cocaine was even an ingredient of Coca Cola until 1903. Opium and opiates were used recreationally in Europe in the nineteenth century. In London alone, there were between 16,000 and 26,000 shops selling opiates during the 1850s.

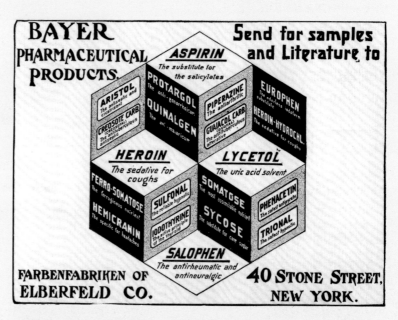

Heroin was released by the Bayer pharmaceutical company in 1898, and aspirin was released a year later. Both products were respectable medical drugs made by similar processes in the same laboratories.

Brand-new drugs

During the twentieth century new synthetic drugs emerged made entirely from chemical ingredients. The first synthesized drug was LSD (lysergic acid diethylamide), made by Albert Hoffman in 1938. LSD is a hallucinogen – it produces vivid, real-seeming illusions that may affect all the senses – and became popular in the 1960s.

Another drug produced in the laboratory is ecstasy (MDMA). It was first produced in 1912 by the German drug company Merck researching blood-clotting agents, but it was ignored until 1976. Then a researcher, Alexander Shulgin, tried it on himself and its recreational use rapidly developed.

New drugs came thick and fast from the middle of the twentieth century. Ketamine was developed as an anaesthetic in the 1960s and was both used and misused by US soldiers during the Vietnam War. Small laboratories producing crystal meth appeared in California in the 1950s and became widespread in the following decades.

Stronger and stronger

Some drugs that have been around for a very long time have recently appeared in more potent forms. Since 1985 cocaine has been processed as crack cocaine – a far more dangerous and addictive drug than cocaine itself. And a strong form of cannabis, called skunk, has been produced by the selective breeding of cannabis plants.

Expert View

'Everything in the room spun around, and the familiar objects and pieces of furniture assumed grotesque, threatening forms. They were in continuous motion, animated, as if driven by an inner restlessness.

'The lady next door . . . was no longer Mrs R, but rather a malevolent, insidious witch with a coloured mask.'

Albert Hoffman's experiment with LSD

US troops fighting the Viet Cong guerrillas in South Vietnam endured terrible conditions. Many used drugs, including the tranquillizer ketamine, to help them cope with the stress and discomfort.

Regulating drugs

In the eighteenth and nineteenth centuries opium use was so widespread in China that the country was in crisis. Users were so desperate that they would sell everything they owned to get opium – even members of their families. The government responded by passing the first drug law, making it illegal to use or sell opium. Western nations have followed the same path in the face of increasing drug use. Smoking opium became illegal in the USA in 1869.

When French troops fighting in Egypt in 1798 discovered cannabis, Napoleon banned its use. Even so, the soldiers brought the habit back to Europe. The use of cannabis in the USA rose following an influx of Mexican cannabis users after the Mexican Revolution in 1910. Public alarm at the rush of immigrants turned to fear and prejudice, leading many states to ban the non-medical use of cannabis from 1915 onwards. A few years earlier, in 1901, a Royal Commission in the UK had declared cannabis an insufficient threat to warrant a ban.

Since the early twentieth century legislation has covered the use, possession and sale of more and more drugs, but sometimes struggles to keep up with the introduction of new types.

Legal and illegal drugs

Whether a drug is legal or illegal is not directly related to how dangerous it is; it is largely historical. Because tobacco and alcohol have been used in Europe and the USA

A Chinese worker in an opium den offers an opium pipe to a female customer. Opium dens sprang up in the Chinatown areas of many cities outside of China. Southeast Asia, North America and France in particular had many opium dens in the nineteenth century.

for a long time, they are legal. It is easier to control a new drug than to restrict the use of one that is already established.

Laws governing drug use vary widely from country to country. Many Muslim countries impose a strict ban on alcohol and have serious penalties for lawbreakers, for example. In the Netherlands using cannabis carries no legal penalty, while in the USA and in much of Europe cannabis use is punishable with fines or even imprisonment. Laws change over time, too – from 1920 to 1933,

FORUM

Is there any hope of dismantling the drugs trade?

No
There will always be a demand for drugs and people willing to supply them. People have used drugs for thousands of years – we can't change that. We're fighting a losing battle, because people want the effects drugs can create.

Yes
We don't have to tolerate bad things just because they are well-established. We tackled slavery, so we can defeat the drugs trade.

What's your opinion?

for example, the sale of alcohol was illegal in the USA.

International law
The Single Convention on Narcotic Drugs (1961) is an international treaty that binds members of the United Nations to an agreement on the supply of and trade in many illegal drugs, including cocaine and opiates made from opium. It is supported by laws in the individual member countries.

An Afghan girl uses a special water pipe to smoke opium. She is sitting at a roadside stall selling opium-smoking equipment.

Chapter 3

What happens today?

Today the trade in drugs spans the globe. It deals in the raw ingredients of drugs, the chemicals needed to process them and the finished product itself. All stages of the production, transport and sale of drugs are illegal.

Growing drug crops

The raw ingredients for many drugs come from plants. The cannabis plant provides cannabis leaves and resin; cocaine comes from the leaves of the coca plant; opium (used to make heroin) comes from the seed heads of the opium poppy.

Cannabis is increasingly grown indoors using hydroponic cultivation techniques. This involves growing plants without any soil, using solutions of nutrients instead. Indoor cultivation makes it difficult for law enforcers to find and destroy cannabis crops. Large-scale production on normal, outdoor farms is an important part of the economy in some countries, such as Morocco and the Lebanon.

Coca is a bush from South America. Much of it is grown on farms on the slopes of the Andes in Colombia, Bolivia and Peru, with Colombia producing most. New leaves are picked from the bushes and dried on mats in the sun before being packed for sale.

Most opium comes from the 'Golden Crescent' – Afghanistan, Pakistan and Iran – and the 'Golden Triangle' – Burma, Laos and Thailand. Afghanistan produced 90 per cent of the world's heroin in 2008. Farm workers

Poppy fields in Kinduz, Afghanistan, produce an opium crop that is sold around the world. Although in some areas security forces seize and destroy crops, there are many places in which farmers grow poppies openly and with little trouble.

Growing cannabis using hydroponic techniques means that the plants can be grown indoors, away from the eyes of police and customs officials. The plants are grown in water with added nutrients under artificial grow-lights that produce plenty of heat.

cut or scratch the unripe seed heads each day for three to five days, allowing the sap to ooze out. The sap is scraped away and dried before being processed into heroin.

Making drugs

Synthetic drugs, such as LSD and ecstasy, are made in laboratories. Many of the ecstasy laboratories are in the Netherlands, Poland and Belgium, with some found in the UK. The equipment needed is not particularly sophisticated, and a laboratory can be set up for around £4,000. Many laboratories are built in the backs of vans so that they can be moved around easily, keeping ahead of the police.

Making LSD is much harder and more dangerous than making ecstasy. It uses dangerous chemicals that can cause poisoning and explosions, and it requires sophisticated equipment and a good knowledge of chemistry. It is made in small batches, but a little goes a very long way: 5 kilograms of LSD can provide 100 million doses.

Making methamphetamine (speed) is straightforward, but dangerous. Around 15 per cent of the meth laboratories discovered are found because accidents have occurred. Meth can be made from standard household products and medicines. Much is made in Mexico and in California, but there are factories around the world, including some floating factories on ships.

FOCUS

Dangerous chemicals
Baby Johna Osborn was only a year old when she was burned in a horrific accident – her parents' meth lab blew up in their home and set fire to the baby's crib. The baby suffered serious burns to more than half her body.

The drugs chain

A long chain of people is involved in producing, processing, moving and supplying a drug. Drugs are smuggled from the countries where they are produced to the countries where they will be used. They are then sold on to local dealers. These dealers may sell them on again, through a chain of ever-smaller deals, until the drug reaches the final user. The dealer at the end of the line often divides the drug into doses, and may sometimes process it further or 'cut' (mix) it with other substances to make it go further, and so make more money, or change its effects.

Why do people grow drug crops?

It's easy to assume that people who grow coca, cannabis or opium poppies for a living are evil criminals. Many of the farmers who produce these crops, though, have little choice. They are driven by economic need — it is the only crop they can grow for which they will be paid enough to feed their families. In some countries the entire national economy depends on drug crops.

Opium growers are often ruthless in defence of their crop – it is, after all, the cash crop they need to feed themselves and their families. This man uses a Kalashnikov rifle to patrol his poppy fields.

Expert View

'Coca is a means of survival for us. Because the soil is very tired, very eroded. Coca leaves are the only option we have for earning a living to feed ourselves and our families.

'We can't substitute it with other products like citrus fruits or coffee. Citrus fruits are very cheap. There are supplies sitting there rotting. I would not be able to feed my family by growing citrus fruits . . .'

Celestino Quispe, peasant farmer in Bolivia

Not all drug farmers are forced by need to grow drugs. In economically developed countries, growing drug crops is a choice. Small-scale growers may wish only to supply their own needs (usually for cannabis) and just sell on any surplus. On a larger scale, drug farmers are motivated by greed. They may give little thought to the misery the drugs trade produces, or they may not care.

Moving drugs

Drugs, and the raw materials and chemicals used to produce them, are smuggled into and out of drug-producing areas. They are moved over land, and by ship, speedboat and plane along the routes that have least security.

Huge volumes of drugs pass through well-established international routes and hubs. About 90 per cent of the cocaine and the majority of other drugs destined for the USA pass through Mexico and Central America. Drugs travelling from Asia to the USA and from South America to Europe, Africa and Asia often pass through Nigeria. Well-used routes include the path taken by heroin from Pakistan and Afghanistan through Iran and Turkey into Europe, and from Burma through China.

Thai police escort Laota Saenlee, who worked for one of the most important Burmese drug barons. He was arrested in Chaing Mai province, Thailand, in 2003.

Smugglers go to great lengths to build secret compartments in vehicles to hide drug shipments. Some use containers carried by commercial shipping lines among hundreds of other containers of legal cargo. Some drug cartels have craft rather like submarines, but that don't go completely underwater, leaving 5–60 centimetres above the surface. They are not easily picked up by radar.

The wreckage of a private light aircraft, which crashed in a swamp while being pursued by US drug-enforcement officers. The pilot was smuggling 360 kg of cannabis from Jamaica when he came down.

Some can travel 8,000 kilometres carrying cocaine around the coast of South America until their illegal cargo is picked up by fast boats and carried to Mexico or the USA.

'Drug mules'

A drug mule is someone who smuggles drugs over an international border. The mule may hide the drugs in a car, motorbike or bag, or on or in his or her body. Some mules

FOCUS

My daughter was a drug mule

Carly Plunkett was jailed for five-and-a-half years for smuggling cocaine into Gambia. She was lured by new 'friends', who took her out and bought her presents and then sent her on a holiday in exchange for running an errand – carrying a case of drugs. Her father said: 'Carly thought it contained weed but was too frightened not to do [it]. She was petrified of the consequences if she didn't go through with it . . . She was only a part-time waitress yet she had a great social life and lots of new clothes. I just wish I'd put two and two together.'

swallow capsules or packages of heroin or cocaine; the drugs are often concealed inside the fingers of latex gloves or in condoms. This is very dangerous – if the package bursts or leaks the mule can die from an overdose. Some mules can swallow 50 to 90 capsules, or about 1.5 kilograms of heroin.

Many mules are recruited among the poor in drug-producing countries, such as Colombia and Mexico. They may earn as much in a single trip as they could earn in a lifetime doing legal work. Others are recruited in Europe and the USA and sent to Africa or South America to bring back drugs. Often they are young people wooed by drug dealers who befriend them and then offer them money to 'run an errand'. Others think it will be an adventure, or they want money to sustain an extravagant lifestyle. Many are feeding their own drug habits and need the money to buy drugs.

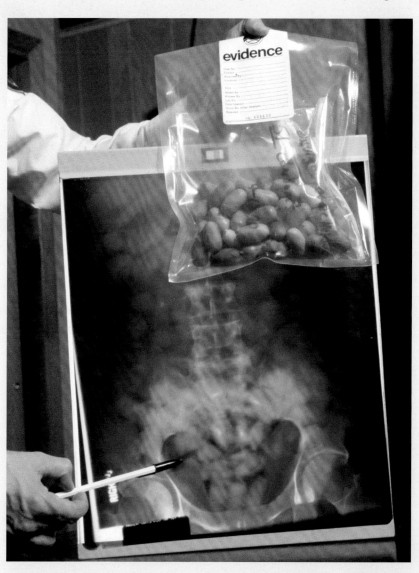

A customs official shows an X-ray of a drug smuggler's intestines clearly showing the narcotic drugs that the smuggler had swallowed. The drugs in the bag above were recovered from the smuggler's system.

Two-way trade

While drugs move out of drug-producing countries, the chemicals used to make them move in the other direction. Chemicals to process opium into heroin, for example, travel from Europe to the Golden Crescent through the Balkan states and Turkey. Those used to make speed travel from the USA into Mexico.

Drugs on the street

When drugs reach the country where they will be used they are sold on to local dealers. Many dealers at the end of the chain sell directly to friends.

Dealers are not the only people working the street in the drugs trade. The informal team includes many young people – some only children – working as lookouts, spotters, couriers and enforcers. Lookouts warn dealers if the police or a rival dealer approaches during a deal. Spotters tell the buyers where to go to pick up their drugs. Couriers carry drugs from place to place and often do not know, or care, what they are carrying. Enforcers are often gang members – their job is to intimidate people who have not paid, and to protect the dealer's territory using violence if necessary. Gang warfare over territories is common. In some cities, it leads to many deaths each year.

Starting to deal

Often, drug users who find that they cannot afford their increasingly expensive drug habit turn to dealing to pay for it. These dealers are driven by desperation and are at the end of the distribution chain. They are least likely to be careful and so most likely

A law-enforcement officer working in Bridgeport, Connecticut, USA, holds a bag of crack cocaine and a $10 note seized as evidence in a drugs raid. The crack cocaine has been broken down into individual street deals.

A drug addict injecting himself. Long-term drug users often have arteries that have become hardened by scar tissue and have to inject into different parts of the body – including the legs, groin, neck and between the toes.

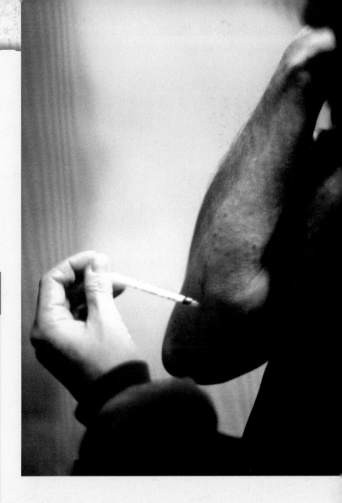

to be picked up by the police. At the top of the dealing chain, people are motivated by greed for profit. They are usually cold and

FORUM

Is being part of the illegal drugs trade a matter of personal choice, or do some people find themselves with no other option? And do we have an obligation to help people who are involved in the drug trade?

Can't help
We can't protect people from themselves. If they want to take drugs, or work as a drug mule, then as long as they are adults there is little we can do to stop them.

Must help
The drug trade preys on desperate people – from farmers through mules to end-users. These are people who have been let down by their society and turn to drugs as a last resort. We must help them, and help to prevent others becoming involved.

What's your opinion?

calculating, fully in control of what they are doing, and often do not use drugs themselves. They are least likely to be caught by the police – but they are the most important ones to arrest.

Making it go further
Drugs are expensive, and they get more so further down the dealing chain as more and more people have taken a profit. To make drugs go further, dealers often cut (or mix) them with other substances. The end-user does not always know this has happened. Sometimes drugs are cut with harmless substances; sometimes they are mixed with other, cheaper drugs or with substances that may be harmful or even dangerous.

Chapter 4

Why fight the drugs trade?

The drugs trade is illegal – but so are many other activities, and they do not attract the same international effort to stamp them out. Why is the drugs trade so important?

The true cost of drugs

Drugs exact a heavy personal and social price, destroying the lives of millions of people around the world. Trading in drugs for profit is a callous, inhumane way to make money and it touches many people. The problem is massive – in South America alone more than a million people are involved in the coca trade.

Some drug users argue that taking drugs is a matter of personal choice. This ignores the impact that the drugs trade has on other people – not just

An official police photograph showing a haul of 670 kg of hashish (which is made from cannabis resin and stalks) that was seized by Pakistani police near the border with Afghanistan in 2009.

the friends, family and community of the drug user, but also the farmers who are intimidated by drug gangs, the mules who are imprisoned for trafficking and the small-time dealers who are shot or beaten by rivals.

Dangers of drug use

Drug misuse can lead to many forms of physical and mental ill-health, and even to death. Addiction leads people to use more and more of a drug to achieve the same effect. Some users eventually overdose, dying or suffering permanent physical or mental damage as a result. Besides the direct effects of drug misuse, there are many related health risks. Using contaminated needles to inject drugs can lead to infection with deadly diseases, such as hepatitis and HIV/AIDS. People under the influence of drugs are more likely to have accidents and may be more likely to take risks and behave foolishly. Sometimes, people hallucinating after using magic mushrooms or LSD have jumped out of high windows believing they could fly. If they drive while under the influence of drugs, people may harm themselves and others. They may have unsafe sex, abuse others or self-harm.

Using contaminated drugs or combining drugs pose an extra danger for the user. If drugs are mixed together they may have a very dangerous effect on the body. If the strength of a drug is not reliable, it is easy for a user to overdose by accident.

The Cartucho ghetto in Bogotá, Colombia, is home to 10,000 homeless people who live with poverty and violence. Many make money from recycling rubbish, but they spend it all on drugs.

Effects on others

The damaging effects of drugs extend beyond the person using the substances. Families are placed under emotional and financial strain by living with or supporting a drug user, and other family members may become physically or mentally ill as a result. While some drug users are able to hold down a job and function normally, many cannot. When they have little money to support themselves, some turn to drug dealing and other criminal activities. The drug scene is steeped in violence and abuse: prostitution, gang violence and many types of street crime result directly from drug dealing.

Social impact

Even people who have no contact with drugs or drug users can be touched by the drugs trade. There is a high financial cost in providing health care and social security payments for drug users, in fighting drug crime and in prosecuting and imprisoning drug users and dealers. This uses state funding that could be spent on other things, such as housing, schools, hospitals and transport networks. Some drug users are not economically productive, reducing the overall wealth of a community or nation.

Areas blighted by drug crime are unpleasant or even dangerous for people to live in. Residents may feel unsafe, threatened by gangs and violent drug dealers or users. The environment may be damaged, with dropped needles making playgrounds unsafe, and

Drug users' hyperdermic needles discarded in public places represent a serious threat to health, particularly to children, who may pick them up without realizing the dangers of infection if they were to prick themselves.

by people urinating in public spaces or vandalizing property. Cleaning up the environment carries a high financial cost, and may have to be frequently repeated. People who cannot afford to leave a run-down area plagued by drug crime may become both mentally and physically ill.

Drugs and crime

Crime is involved in the drugs trade at all stages of production, distribution, sale and use. In South America there are frequent gun battles over coca plantations as warring drug barons fight to take control of the supply. The farm workers are pawns in this, often becoming victims of the violence, but with no say in who they work for. Drug crime accounts for a lot of crime overall in many countries. About 75 per cent of the people in prison in the USA, for example, have been convicted of drug-related crimes.

Colombian coca grower Wilmar Ospina tends his coca plants. His crop had been almost wiped out four months previously by a plane commissioned by the USA to spray and destroy coca crops.

FOCUS

Innocent victim

Eileen Mohan's son Christopher was 22 when he was shot by gangsters in 2007. The armed gangs in Vancouver, Canada, fight for control of the trade in synthetic drugs and execute troublesome members within their own gangs. Eileen and her son lived in an apartment opposite a drug dealer and gangster. She says: '[The dealer] compromised our safety and security just by living across from us and the price we paid was that drug dealers came and targeted him to kill him. My son was . . . killed along the way too.'

The cartels and drug barons often engage in gang warfare and many are also involved in other crimes, such as arms trading and money laundering, protection rackets and kidnapping. Some of these are large-scale crimes that tie up national security forces. In some areas the power of the drug

Part of a haul of guns, drugs, money and jewellery on display in Mexico City in 2007. All were seized during several drugs busts. Some of the weapons shown here are gold-plated submachine guns.

barons even influences the political stability of the whole country. Drug cartels may control or finance rebels or guerrillas undermining the authority of the government, or they may be secretly supported or tolerated by the government.

New recruits

Drug smugglers, mules and street dealers work on the front line – many are picked up by the police, and some are killed in fights between drug gangs. This means that new

FORUM

With a limited amount of money, choices always have to be made about how it is spent. The views below are typical of those expressed by people on both sides of the argument:

People who use drugs have made their choice. Instead of spending money on them, and on fighting drugs abroad, we should leave them to it and spend the money on schools, hospitals, roads – things that benefit people who have not chosen to use drugs.

Drugs blight the lives of millions of people. No price is too high – we must crush the drugs trade. Every day, more children are drawn into drugs. There is no more urgent problem.

What's your opinion?

dealers, smugglers, traffickers and gang members must be recruited. Recruiting others to work in the drugs trade is an important link in the chain of crime. Dealers recruit new users, too. They might go to schools and give free drugs to children, encouraging them to try drugs in the hope of getting them hooked. To protect future generations from falling into drug misuse, joining gangs and starting out on a life of crime it is important to step in and break the chain.

Expert View

'During [the 1990s, when US-backed forces tried to eradicate coca growing in Bolivia], I would receive an average of ten complaints a day from coca growers. Murders, rapes, robberies, assaults, all of that, committed by soldiers and police against the growers.'

Godofredo Reinecke, former Chapare human rights ombudsman in Bolivia

Not just us

It is easy for people in the economically developed countries at the end of the drugs chain to forget those at the other end of the chain who are also victims of the drugs trade. Many people who work to grow drugs live in abject poverty, many are themselves addicted to drugs, and often they are subjected to violence as drug barons fight over the farmland and as enforcers seize and destroy their crops. The drugs trade also harms the mules who smuggle drugs over borders, who risk imprisonment, execution and death from accidents with the drugs they carry.

A drug dealer being arrested by police in the Watts district of Los Angeles, California. The police are only too well aware that to make a real impact on the illegal drugs trade they need to remove the major players.

Chapter 5

What are we doing about the drugs trade?

Worldwide there are up to 200 million users of illegal drugs, so tackling the drugs trade is an enormous task. There are two broad approaches: coming down hard on suppliers and users, and trying to reduce the use of drugs by educating and rehabilitating users.

Why is the problem so hard to tackle?

Entrenched political problems, poverty, powerful and greedy drug cartels and desperate users combine to make the drugs trade very difficult for governments and security forces to combat. Opium and coca are grown in countries with complex social and political problems. Rebels fighting against established governments need funds, and drugs provide an easy way of raising money. Tackling drug farming involves taking on the political problems and poverty in these volatile and difficult areas.

Politics and poppies

The Taliban is an Islamic political and religious movement that is powerful in Afghanistan and Pakistan – both important opium-producing areas. Until 2001 the Taliban governed

The Taliban destroying a crop of opium poppies in Afghanistan. Although the Taliban once took a strict anti-drug stance, since being forced out of power it has taken to funding its operations with money from drug farming and dealing.

Police with sniffer dogs check a line of stationary vehicles for drugs in Texas, USA. Drug smugglers frequently cross the land border that separates Mexico and the United States with concealed shipments of cocaine.

Afghanistan. In 2000 they clamped down on opium farming in the country, burning heroin factories and insisting farmers destroy poppy crops. By 2001 opium farming in important poppy-producing regions had been almost eradicated. But also in 2001 allied forces led by the USA and the UK drove the Taliban from power. Opium production returned to its normal levels in only a year. The Taliban now uses profits from opium farming to support its guerrilla activities in the area.

In other areas the government might turn a blind eye to drug production, or even encourage it. For example, only 1 per cent of the opium produced in Burma is stopped before it leaves the country. The government of Venezuela is helping Bolivian coca farmers to process and sell their drug, and is even helping to build coca-processing plants.

FOCUS

Coca entrepreneur
Christo Deneumostier owns the Coca Shop in Cusco, Peru, where he sells coca cookies, pastries and even coca ice cream. He says he wants to become the 'Starbucks of coca', opening Coca Shop franchises throughout Peru and abroad. He uses coca flavouring, but not cocaine. He hopes to build the legal market for coca, which may help Peruvian coca farmers.

Big business
Drug cartels are organizations that work together to control the supply and price of drugs. Some are as large as national governments and their influence spans the globe. They are heavily involved in crime and often linked with arms trading, terrorist groups or insurgents. They often have a stranglehold over a local economy, and might bribe or infiltrate the security services or be in league with corrupt governments.

Working against drugs

The World Health Organization (WHO) and other international bodies work together, often with help from national governments. The USA has taken a leading role in the 'war on drugs', providing funds and troops. It has intervened in Panama and Colombia to cut coca farming as well as working to eradicate opium farming. The Indian government has intervened in opium poppy farming in India itself and elsewhere in the Golden Crescent.

National governments act in their own territories to pursue drug smugglers and dealers. In drug-producing countries a tough stance can have a huge impact. When the Peruvian government gave orders to shoot down the planes carrying coca to refining plants, the output of cocaine from Peru dropped by 40 per cent in five years.

A group of men prepares to burn dried coca leaves during a Bolivian drug-control programme. This was part of 18 tonnes of cocaine seized in Sacaba, Bolivia.

Regulating production

Seizing harvests and destroying farms reduces output, but it has a serious impact on the local economy. It is better if farmers can be persuaded to grow different crops. In South America, the USA and United Nations have provided money to help local farmers move to producing legal crops, such as coffee, bananas, pineapple and citrus fruits, and to help defeat the rebels and criminal gangs who protect the coca crops. But this does not always work, as farmers cannot make as much money from growing these types of food crops.

Changing the nature of the problem

Drug producers do not give in easily under pressure to stop production. Measures that appear to be effective sometimes just lead to different problems. As large coca farms

Expert View

'What the drug war has done is to drive the price of drugs up, so the more the price[s] of drugs go up, the more money there is to corrupt people.'

Col. Trevor McMillan, Jamaican Police

are destroyed in Bolivia and Colombia, for example, production just shifts to tiny plots cultivated in the middle of thick jungle. In Burma and other Golden Triangle countries, the crackdown on opium farming and heroin production has led to increased investment in producing methamphetamine instead. In Mexico the government used troops to fight drug crime in 2008 and arrested or killed the leaders of some cartels. The response was an increase in violence, with 6,000 drug-related murders in that year.

Tackling drugs in transit

Drug smugglers have many ways of moving their illicit shipments around the world. Security forces work with intelligence reports passed between nations to intercept known cargoes, and rely on informers inside the drugs trade for tip-offs. They also patrol sea routes and intercept boats suspected of carrying drugs. A high-speed boat travelling at night under the protection of darkness will always arouse suspicion. Overland routes are patrolled and guarded, using barbed-wire fences, machine-gun points and armed guards to try to stop smugglers, who are often as heavily armed themselves.

Tasmania grows around 50% of the legal opium produced in the world. The low population density and low crime rate in Tasmania make it a relatively safe place to grow poppies for medicinal opium.

Border guards search individuals or vehicles if they suspect drug smuggling. They use a combination of technology and careful observation to find hidden drugs. Sniffer dogs and sniffer robots can also detect the scent of drugs, and X-ray machines and scanners pick up swallowed or hidden packages (see page 21).

Money laundering

Drug cartels make a huge amount of money, but before they can use this money they need to 'launder' it. This means putting it through legal businesses so that it cannot be traced back to drugs or any other criminal activities. Large criminal gangs often run seemingly respectable businesses, such as cafés and shops – businesses that deal with cash and so can take in 'dirty' money and pass it out into legitimate bank accounts.

Preventing money laundering challenges the cartels' ability to use the money they gain from trading in drugs. Fighting this involves using computer technology and trained financial staff to identify suspect transactions and businesses.

Working undercover

Police sometimes work undercover, posing as drug dealers to infiltrate the organizations they are investigating. It is dangerous work – if they are discovered, they will more than likely be killed. Similarly, drug cartels try to infiltrate the police and customs services. In some countries where income is low, parts of the security forces and some government officials are corrupt and work in the pay of the drug cartels to undermine efforts to curb their activities.

Prison officers in Thailand place blindfolds on a convicted murderer and a drugs dealer at Bang Kwang Central Prison, in Bangkok, shortly before they were both executed by lethal injection.

Police exercising their stop-and-search powers at London's annual Notting Hill Carnival. Venues such as this are a magnet for illegal activities, from knife crime and muggings to drug dealing.

Drugs on the street

Picking up drug dealers in the community relies again on a combination of tip-offs and inside information and observation. The police learn where dealers operate, who the local dealers and drug workers are, and step in to arrest them when they are most likely to obtain a successful conviction. It is dangerous work, as many dealers are controlled by vicious crime rings or gangsters and violent confrontations are common.

Police attend events where they know drugs will be used, such as music festivals and carnivals. They plan operations to 'bust' crack-houses and other venues where people gather to deal in and use drugs. In most cases, though, these yield only small amounts of drugs and rarely lead back to the important players in the drug chain.

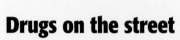

Expert View

'Twenty years ago I arrived as a teacher. There was no school, no road, no agricultural products, just coca, violence, poverty and malnutrition. I was able to persuade authorities to provide a hectare of land to the community so we could grow food. Later on, we started growing coffee . . . When [stubborn] coca growers had their coca eradicated, they left the area and we were able to live more peacefully and productively.'

Severa Bejarano, community leader from Tingo Maria, Colombia

After specialized analysis and enhancement, photographs taken from orbiting satellites, tasked with surveying known drug-growing regions, clearly show suspicious growth patterns on the ground. These areas will require investigation by officers on the ground.

High-tech methods

Drug cartels use the latest technology and the security forces need to match it in order to battle the drugs trade. The security forces use satellite photography and GPS (global-positioning systems) to spot and track drug harvests. They intercept mobile phone and MSN traffic, and use bugs to record conversations.

Patrolling borders is dangerous, so passing on more of the work to technological aids helps to save lives. The construction of a 'virtual fence' along the border between the USA and Mexico is an example of technology being harnessed to help the border patrol force. The fence, only partly built so far, consists of towers equipped with radar, infrared cameras and sensors to detect the movement of people over the border. It can tell people and animals apart, and directs patrols to the places where breaches of the border are taking place. It supplements the real fence which is being built along the border.

Robots play a part in investigating the many tunnels that have been dug under the Mexico–USA border. These tunnels are very dangerous for guards to search, so 'tunnelbots' – remotely controlled robots – are used instead. The tunnelbots use lasers to navigate; they map the tunnels and they also have sensors to pick up any chemical traces of drugs.

Expert View

'[Fighting coca production] has had social costs, and it's very hard to say that coca can be eradicated. Is it useful? Is it sound? Is it a good policy? Are they also eradicating drug consumption? If not, people will start using other drugs.'

Roberto Laserna, Professor of Social Science at Universidad Mayor de San Simón, Cochabamba, Bolivia

Working with drug users

Alongside the hard-line assault on the supply chain of drugs, some countries also target end-users and potential users, using education to dissuade them from taking drugs. Rehabilitation programmes rather than prosecution, and legal substitutes for illegal drugs, help dependent users wean themselves off street drugs. Heavy drug users may remain dependent on some form of drug for a long time, but they are lifted out of the criminal underworld and given assistance in adjusting their lifestyle and managing their drug habit. Removing users from the end of the chain reduces the market for drugs and so undermines the entire drugs trade. Rehabilitation programmes can work alongside punishment, with prisoners convicted of drug-related crimes forced to undergo treatment as part of their penalty.

Worshippers pray for healing during a service at the Christian Betel Centro Drug Rehabilitation Ministry in Madrid, Spain. Most of the participants are recovering heroin users and between 70 and 80% of them have HIV/AIDS.

Chapter 6

What else can we do?

In the long term, the very difficult problems of poverty and political turmoil must be addressed if there is to be any hope of dismantling the drugs trade. In the short term, we need new tactics to reduce the availability of drugs on the street.

Two approaches

There are two broad approaches to the drug problem. One is to take a tough stand, severely punishing drug dealers, farmers and users. The other is to follow a more liberal approach, relying on education, subsidies to farmers to grow other crops, social measures to alleviate poverty and rehabilitation clinics to help users. Although both approaches have some local impact, the global drugs trade has not been reduced in the 40 years since the start of the international 'war on drugs' launched by US president Richard Nixon. Some people are suggesting new approaches that might have more impact.

Confronting dealers

Some North American cities have tested a new approach to the drugs trade that hinges on a meeting between law enforcers and criminals. Project Ceasefire began in Cincinnati in the USA in 2007 to tackle gangland killings. The police insisted that all known gangsters on parole or probation attend

Small-time drug dealer Jamal, seen here in Brooklyn, New York, habitually carries a gun while dealing on the streets. His friend, nicknamed Craze, is wheelchair-bound after a shooting incident.

Two coffee growers transport their crop by mule, covering 6.5 km of rough ground before they reach a dirt road. Increasing problems for farmers of legal crops mean that more of them now turn to violence or growing drugs to make ends meet.

a meeting where they were told that shootings must end now or everyone present would be punished. The murder rate dropped by half in a year. Other cities took up the strategy, and some have applied it directly to drug dealing. In High Point, North Carolina, an open-air drugs market had survived years of police attempts to close it, but the day after the police called drug dealers to a meeting the market disappeared for good.

Legalizing drugs

Some people believe the way to tackle drug misuse is to make the drugs legal, removing the illegal trade and enabling people to seek help without fear of prosecution. It is a complex issue. Decriminalizing dangerous drugs may reduce the crime and violence associated with the drugs trade. It also allows regulation of the supply and quality control of drugs so that fewer people suffer the ill effects of contaminated drugs or variable strengths. At the same time, however, decriminalizing drugs may increase problem drug use, since it gives the message that using drugs is acceptable. People who might have avoided drugs because they were afraid of the law might take up drug use.

Expert View

'The flow of drugs from Latin America into the US and Europe has increased. I think that prohibition has aggravated the problem and it is time to look for new alternatives.'

Cesar Gaviria, former president of Colombia

What happens when a drug is banned?

In the 1920s alcohol was controlled by law in the USA. The manufacture, sale and transportation of alcohol for consumption were all banned. Immediately an underground market in 'bootleg' alcohol sprang up, some of it dangerously strong or contaminated. People went to secret bars to drink, and gangsters dominated the illegal trade. These are all features of the illegal trade in drugs today.

Alcohol is now legal for adults in the USA. It kills around 85,000 people a year, while fewer than 20,000 die from illegal drugs. Legalizing drugs may reduce crime but increase deaths as more people take up drug use. Tobacco, another legal drug, kills around 435,000 people in the USA each year.

What happens when a drug is legalized?

In the Netherlands people can use cannabis without fear of punishment. Its use is widespread, and other Europeans go to Amsterdam to visit the 'coffee shops' where cannabis may be bought and smoked.

The UK government has changed the legal status of cannabis twice. In 2004 it was reclassified as a class C drug, with reduced penalties for possession and use, but in 2009 it was returned to class B, with increased penalties. The government gave as its reason the increased use of a stronger form, known as skunk.

A poster in Ho Chi Minh City, Vietnam, warning against drug use. Heroin is a particular problem in Vietnam.

Education and the media

Educating people about the effects of drug use and misuse may discourage young people from using drugs. But campaigns have to compete with messages in song lyrics and movies that show drug use as being cool, grown-up and rebellious.

FORUM

There are different views about whether or not drugs such as heroin, cocaine and crystal meth should be legal:

In favour

We can reduce the public health damage caused by cocaine by legalizing it – thereby rescuing addicts from the high prices and the many troubles of the black market.

Against

Legalizing drugs gives the message that it's all right to use dangerous drugs. Many people assume that something is safe if it is legal.

What's your opinion?

It is difficult to make advertising with a negative message have a real impact. This is because we naturally reject messages that tell us not to do something. But young people who might not respond to a warning about their own health will often think again if they see the terrible consequences their actions have on others. Many young people have a strong sense of social justice and concern for people in developing countries. Making them aware of the impact their actions have in these areas can be a strong incentive for changing behaviour.

Vinnie Marino, known as the Yoga King of Los Angeles, took up teaching yoga after recovering from drug dependency. By 2009, when this photograph was taken, he had been drug-free for more than 20 years.

Chapter 7

Where next in the war on drugs?

It will take a long time and massive international cooperation to tackle the causes of the drugs trade – poverty, political turmoil and the personal motives that drive people to take drugs. At the same time, we need to continue working with users, and the young people who may grow up into users, to turn them away from dangerous drug use.

Helping users

Without users the drugs trade will fall apart. Many countries have now decided that criminalizing users is not always the best way to combat escalating drug use and have set up schemes to treat users, to help them reduce their need for drugs, or to stay safe while using them.

Needle-exchange programmes allow intravenous drug users to swap used needles for clean ones, so avoiding the infectious diseases they may get from dirty needles. Providing replacement drugs, such as methadone, under medical supervision helps dependent drug users to manage their lifestyle without using street drugs. Rehabilitation centres help users to give up drugs in a safe and supported environment with the necessary medical assistance on hand.

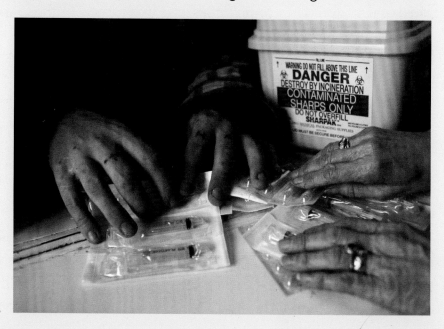

A health worker prepares sterile needles for distribution to drug users at a needle-exchange centre in Cheshire, England. Schemes such as this greatly reduce the incidence of infection from addicts using dirty needles.

This scene – Polish and German border police working together – would have been common before Poland became part of the EU in 2004. However, the removal of border checks means that they no longer mount joint operations, making it easier for drugs to move across Europe.

Changing patterns

While economically developed nations tackle drug use, it expands into other areas. As resistance to the drugs trade grows in the original markets of Western Europe and North America, the drug cartels concentrate on new markets where there is no established policy and procedures for battling the trade. Some African nations are rapidly developing better transport and information infrastructures, but still have many people living in desperate poverty. These people are vulnerable to drug misuse and drugs are flooding in. Drug problems are increasing rapidly in sub-Saharan Africa, Russia and Eastern Europe. Less economically developed countries cannot afford the resources to tackle the drugs trade used in wealthier countries, so drug cartels can work easily in these areas.

Information technology

New information technology is making it easier to give support to drug users as well as to trace dealers. Online groups help people to keep in touch with others who can help and support them at any time of the day or night. An instant-messaging chat service called MXit is being used in Cape Town, South Africa, to communicate with drug users in a way they are comfortable with.

Listening to all

The move towards more open government that has come with the rise of the Internet means that governments in some countries are consulting with more and more people as they revise their drugs policies. Instead of working only with politicians and experts, they are now open to input from police officers, drug users and others involved in the problem.

Glossary

active ingredient The chemical in a drug that has an effect on the body.

alkaloid A naturally occurring chemical containing nitrogen that is found in some medicines as well as in recreational drugs such as cocaine.

bootleg An illegally produced or sold product. The term can apply to illegally recorded music, but it is most often associated with the prohibition era in the USA in the 1920s and 1930s, when the manufacture, transportation and sale of alcohol was illegal.

drug cartel A large criminal organization that deals in drugs.

cocaine Drug made from the leaves of the coca bush.

contaminated drug A drug that contains impurities.

crack cocaine A refined and more potent form of cocaine.

crack-house A place where crack cocaine is made, sold or used.

crystal meth Methamphetamine hydrochloride, a highly addictive drug used as a stimulant.

drug baron A person who runs or plays a major role in a large drug trafficking organization, often across national borders.

ecstasy A synthetic recreational drug sold in tablet form. It is often referred to as being a 'party drug'.

eradication Completely wiping something out.

GPS Global positioning system – a method for working out the location of an object by calculating its position in relation to satellites orbiting the planet.

guerrilla war Unconventional warfare waged by small groups making surprise hit-and-run or terror attacks.

heroin A drug that is made from refined opium, a substance that comes from particular varieties of poppies.

ketamine An anaesthetic that can also be misused as a recreational drug.

leper Person with leprosy – a disease that attacks the nerves, skin, eyes and limbs. If this disease is left untreated it causes permanent damage.

LSD Lysergic acid diethylamide, a synthetic drug supplied on pieces of impregnated paper. Minute amounts of the drug cause vivid hallucinations when ingested.

magic mushrooms A naturally occurring fungus that causes hallucinations when eaten.

methamphetamine Also known as 'speed', a synthetic drug used as a stimulant.

morphine A painkiller made from opium poppies.

mule A person who, knowingly or unknowingly, smuggles drugs over an international border. Paid mules are often poor people who receive relatively little for the dangers they run.

nutrients Chemicals that are needed to nourish a plant or animal.

opiate A chemical drug made from opium.

opium A drug derived from the sap of opium poppies.

pharmaceutical Relating to medical drugs.

rehabilitation Recovering a healthy lifestyle by defeating addiction or leaving a life of crime behind.

skunk A strong form of cannabis.

speed Another name for methamphetamine.

Taliban A militant political and fundamentalist Islamic group active in Afghanistan and Pakistan.

trafficker Someone who moves drugs around for sale.

volatile substance A substance that evaporates at a low temperature.

Further information

Books

Chasing the High: A Firsthand Account of One Young Person's Experience with Substance Abuse by Kyle Keegan and Howard Moss, Annenberg Foundation Trust, 2008

Drug Culture (In The News) by A Smith, Franklin Watts, 2003

Drugs Trade (Just the Facts) by Jim McGuigan, Heinemann, 2005

The Drugs Trade (21st Century Debates) by Louie Fooks, Wayland, 2003

Junk by Melvin Burgess, Puffin, 1996

Real Life Heroes: Stories about Surviving Drug Addicition by Paul Mason, Franklin Watts, 2010

Films

http://edition.cnn.com/2009/CRIME/04/16/creative.drug.smugglers/index.html#cnnSTCVideo

A CNN video showing how drug smugglers get drugs into the USA and how customs officials try to stop them.

Maria Full of Grace, 2004, directed by Joshua Marston

A feature film about a young, pregnant drugs mule smuggling cocaine out of Colombia; UK 15; USA R rating.

Websites

http://news.bbc.co.uk/hi/english/static/in_depth/world/2000/drugs_trade/production/holland.stm

An in-depth guide to the world trade in drugs of all types.

http://www.guardian.co.uk/society/series/drugs-uncovered

A collection of articles on the drugs trade.

http://www.talktofrank.com/

UK government site on different drugs and the drugs trade.

http://www.pbs.org/wgbh/pages/frontline/shows/drugs/

A history of the US war against drugs.

Index

Entries in **bold** are for pictures.